Marc A. Bauch

# "Gentlemen, Be Seated!"

## The Rise and the Fall of the Minstrel Show

**Document Nr. V183957**

**Marc A. Bauch**

# "Gentlemen, Be Seated!"

## The Rise and the Fall of the Minstrel Show

GRIN Verlag

Bibliografische Information der Deutschen Nationalbibliothek: Die Deutsche Bibliothek verzeichnet diese Publikation in der Deutschen Nationalbibliografie; detaillierte bibliografische Daten sind im Internet über http://dnb.d-nb.de/ abrufbar.



**1. Auflage 2011**

**http://www.grin.com**
**Druck und Bindung: Books on Demand GmbH, Norderstedt Germany**
**ISBN 978-3-656-08636-9**

# "Gentlemen, Be Seated!"

## The Rise and the Fall of the Minstrel Show

by

Marc A. Bauch

# Preface

> We wear the mask that grins and lies,
> It hides our cheeks and shades our eyes –
> This debt we pay to human guile;
> With torn and bleeding hearts we smile
> And mouth with myriad subtleties.
> from: "We Wear the Masks" by Paul Laurence Dunbar (1872-1906)

In America, there was no aristocracy to finance playwrights, actors, and theaters. America was a good ground for self-funding, commercial and light entertainment. Several subgenres of theater developed in the US in the 19th century: the minstrel show, ballad opera, burlesque, extravaganza, vaudeville, operetta, the revue and musical comedy, which all assimilated into the American musical in the 20th century.

A native form of entertainment that came up around 1843 was the minstrel show. The minstrel show was a show that consisted of melodies by Negro slaves and jokes by white actors in blackface in order to imitate the blacks. Led by Mr. Interlocutor, the master of ceremonies, three more actors in blackface sat in a semicircle. The endmen or cornermen were known as Mr. Bones and Mr. Tambo, who joked together or made fun of the Negro slaves. Thus, the minstrel show was double-edged: on the one hand, racism in the United States was reinforced; on the other hand, so many white Americans have come aware of black popular culture. No wonder therefore, the rise of the minstrel show coincided with the growth of the abolitionist movement in the 19th century. But without doubt, racial discrimination was played down in the minstrel show. The minstrel show was meant as a form of entertainment, which was not intended to be taken seriously. Although the minstrel aimed to create a native and distinctly American form of entertainment, the songs they adopted were of English, Irish or

Scottish origin. Furthermore, they presented parodies of European-style entertainment or parodied works by William Shakespeare. In this book, I will present the history of the minstrel show.

I wish my readers, when reading the book, a part of the pleasure that I had during the project on this unique genre and while writing this book about the genesis and development of a more or less native form of American entertainment and a distinctively American contribution to theatrical history.

Hermeskeil, Germany, December 2011 Marc A. Bauch

# Table of Contents

1. The Origins of the Minstrel Show and Its European Antecedents ..... 5
2. Jim Crow and Zip Coon ..... 10
3. Banjo Music and Dance ..... 18
4. Daniel D. Emmet and the Virginia Minstrels ..... 23
5. The Hey-Day of the Minstrel Show ..... 30
6. The Decline of the Minstrel Show ..... 36
7. The Cultural Importance of the Minstrel Show and Its Legacy ..... 40
8. Bibliography ..... 43

# "Gentlemen, Be Seated!"

## The Rise and the Fall of the Minstrel Show

by

Marc A. Bauch

# 1. The Origins of the Minstrel Show and Its European Antecedents

One milestone in the history of 19th century American theater is the minstrel show. As the only uniquely American genre within American theater, the minstrel show is the most important antecedent of the American musical and influenced musicals like *Porgy and Bess* (1935).

"The minstrel show was a unique development, a purely native form of entertainment, and a distinctively American contribution to theatrical history."[1] This is how Carl Wittke judges about popular stage entertainment in the US, where whites imitated black slaves in song and dance.[2] In the minstrel show, blacks were portrayed and mocked. White actors blacked their faces with burnt cork and carried wigs with curly hair. In sketches, songs and dances, Negro slaves were shown as decayed, superstitious, happy and musical characters. The minstrel show is a turning point in American theater, because after the second War of Independence against England from 1812 to 1814 the Americans wanted to become independent, not only politically, but also with respect to culture: "The minstrel show was the most important new form."[3]

Already in European theater, there were dark figures: In ancient drama, the Greeks had their "phallophoroi". Demons, goblins, Indians,

---

[1] Carl F. Wittke, *Tambo and Bones: A History of the American Minstrel Stage* (Durham, 1930), p. vii.

[2] As race, discrimination and segregation play an important part in American theater, for example in the minstrel show, I will use for clarification the expressions whites, colored, blacks, negroes, etc., although today in avoidance of discrimination other concepts are usually used, for example African-Americans. But that is what the situation was like in those days. No evaluation is intended with the use of these concepts and expressions.

[3] Robert C. Toll, *Blacking Up: The Minstrel Show in Nineteenth-Century America* (New York, 1974), p. 4.

Turks, moors and blacks can be found in Renaissance Theater. Also William Shakespeare's *Othello* is such a representation of a black character. Pulcinella and Arlecchino are two swarthy characters of the Commedia dell'Arte.[4] On European stages, blacks were already shown as imitations of Africans. At the end of the 17th century, also on American stages black-faced actors appeared who played minor roles as servants and who were provided for comic relief.

The models for the minstrel show are younger. They look back to a comic embodiment of blacks by whites in the opera buffa. These artificial blacks were often evil or unpleasant characters; however, no form of discrimination was intended. These imitations were to serve merely for entertainment. The English composer Charles Dibdin became interested in "Negro Songs".[5] In 1768, Charles Dibdin composed *The Padlock*, an opera in which the composer himself played a black. Dibdin used a language which imitated a dialect of the blacks in songs composed by Dibdin himself, but otherwise he neither used elements of African music nor even American music as performed by blacks. His songs stand in the tradition of the Italian opera.[6] Even the picture on the next page shows Dibdin as a classical opera singer. Dibdin was known throughout the US, for example, Herman Melville refers to him in the third chapter of his *Billy Budd, Sailor*.

---

[4] Cf. Hans Nathan, *Dan Emmett and the Rise of Early Negro Minstrelsy* (Norman, 1962), p. 3.

[5] Ibid., p. 20.

[6] Cf. ibid., p. 22.

Between 1815 and 1830, the first native images came up in which white actors caricatured the blacks in dance, singing and action. The presentation of American slaves on stage outlined neither a real image of African-Americans, nor a real picture of their situation. They were caricatured: “images of Negroes were shaped by white expectations and desires and not by black realities."[7] The minstrel show was meant as a form of entertainment, which was not intended to be taken seriously. The faces colored with burnt cork had the function of masks.[8] With the second War of Independence against England in 1812, the Americans wanted to become culturally independent. This war led to a turning point in American literature, especially in American Theater. With a growing national political consciousness of the young republic, American theater also gained a growing national consciousness which was expressed by American themes. More and more, the American playwright distanced himself from European models and used American topics and American locales: "After the war of 1812, when the quest for a distinctly American culture dominated the arts, however, blackfaced characters became increasingly Afro-American."[9] For the dramatization of American topics, the blacks were ideal types, at least for imitation and caricature. The black character in European drama was substituted by a more realistic representation of a local African-American. The American counterpart was developed to a funny type. With his falsetto voice and his trailing, sluggish walk the American stage character of the comical black was an incessant component in American theater. The blackface character complemented the stage Yankee and the Frontiersman. Charles Mathews, George Washington Dixon and Edwin Forrest gained fame by their parodies of the African-American; Forrest was so successful with his role that one could hardly distinguish him from an African-

---

[7] Toll, *Blacking Up: The Minstrel Show in Nineteenth-Century America*, p. vi.

[8] Cf. ibid., p. 200.

[9] Ibid., p. 26.

American when he walked through the streets. He was so good that he could even fool blacks when he mingled with them.[10]

[10] Cf. Mel Watkins, *On the Real Side: Laughing, Lying, and Signifying: The Underground Tradition of African-America Humor that Transformed American Culture* (New York, 1994), p. 83.

## 2. Jim Crow and Zip Coon

The songs and the dances of the slaves brought a stir even before the Civil War. The tightening of a leg was characteristic of their dance steps. Their songs which they accompanied on a guitar or a banjo are full of humor and pathos.[11] From these sources, the American minstrel drew his repertoire and he developed a caricature of the African-American. The minstrel often came from the Northern States or they were foreign immigrants who had their ideas of the black plantation worker only by hearsay.[12] Two stage types developed. On the one hand, it was the urban dandy type that was overly and modernly dressed and he was humorous. On the other hand, the stage type of the lazy and careless southern Negro emerged, who drifted around and had a fondness for watermelons.[13]

> […] the plantation type which got into minstrelsy apparently was calculated to give the impression that all Negroes were lazy, shiftless fellows, careless of the morrow. The stage Negro loved watermelons and ate them in a peculiar way. He turned out to be an expert wielder of the razor, a weapon which he always had ready for use on such special social occasions as crap games, of which the stage Negro was passionately fond.[14]

We find the black expert with the razor also in other genres of 19th century American Literature, for example in Herman Melville's *Benito Cereno*

---

[11] The banjo is an African instrument which is to play an important role in American folklore: "the African slaves brought to America a musical instrument that subsequently became so important in our folklore." (Gilbert Chase, *America's Music* (New York, 1955), p. 67)

[12] Cf. Wittke, op. cit., p. 40.

[13] Other types like the Mammy, the Old Darky, the provocative Mulatto wench and the black soldier were developed, as well. The Mulatto wench was called „Lucy Long":

> Miss Lucy she is handsome,
> And Miss Lucy she is tall,
> And de way she spreads her ankles,
> Is death to the niggers all. (quoted in: Wittke, op. cit., p. 180)

[14] Wittke, op. cit., p. 8.

(1855). Between 1820 and 1840, however, there were two types of characters in the minstrelsy: the plantation type and the urban dandy type. The awkward ragged plantation worker became known as Jim Crow by Thomas D. Rice.

The most famous of all minstrel show performers, was born in New York in 1808 and was given the name "Daddy Rice". He was a strolling actor and traveled to Ohio, Kentucky and Tennessee. In 1828, Rice bridged the gap between the acts of Solon Robinson's *The Rifle* when he appeared as Jim Crow: "It was an interpolation between the acts of this play that Rice first sang and jumped 'Jim Crow'".[15]

Rice once observed how a humpback African-American with a deformed shoulder scavenged the road while buzzing a funny song and cut a caper to the refrain. His right shoulder was slanted upwards and he suffered from rheumatism, which explains his strange dance steps.

> One day while Rice was walking through the streets of one of these Middle Western towns, Louisville in all probability, or perhaps along its river front, he encountered an old slave crooning an old melody and doing a curious shuffling step each time he reached the chorus of his little song. According to one account, the Negro was cleaning and rubbing down the horses in the stable-yard near the Louisville theatre where Rice was then playing. The original Jim Crow must have been a curious and interesting figure, a strange mixture of pathos and humor. His right shoulder was deformed and drawn up high; his left leg was gnarled with rheumatism, stiff and crooked at the knee, so that the Negro walked with a limp, obviously painful and yet laughable. As he worked, he sang a rather mournful tune and, at the end of each stanza, gave a queer little jump, setting his 'heel-a-rickin' as he alighted.[16]

---

[15] Wittke, op. cit., p. 23.

The expression Jim Crow Laws goes back to Rice's performance (cf. C. Vann Woodward, *The Strange Career of Jim Crow* (New York, 1955), p. 7).

[16] Wittke, op. cit., pp. 24-25.

The melody of the song "Jump Jim Crow" is a traditional Irish folk song.[17] Rice aped the African-American in dress and attitude as Jim Crow and memorized the song. This Jim Crow song was supplemented by many stanzas, but the chorus remained the same:

> First on the heel tap, den on de toe,
> Ebery time I wheel about I jump Jim Crow,
> Wheel about and turn about and do jis so,
> And every time I wheel about I jump Jim Crow.[18]

In his song, the performer self-reflexively describes his own dance. Also linguistically and rhetorically, the recurring character of the dance is highlighted by epanalepses and the rhyme scheme. The speech rhythm imitates his dance. It consists of dactyls and hemiola which slow down the rhythm. The register of the language is an exaggerated imitation of African-American vernacular. Thomas Dartmouth "Daddy" Rice created a sensational success with his Jim Crow figure and his song gained increasing popularity.

The role of Jim Crow was not a defined role. Rice turned down his role again and again and added comments and hints on current and local events to his song. In 1832, Rice had a sensational success with his role as Jim Crow in New York's Bowery Theatre. The audience clapped him out twenty times. Not only in America, the Jim Crow song was also a success in London, where Rice appeared on stage in 1836.[19] Rice was such a success that *The Boston Post* wrote: "The two most popular characters in the

---

[17] Cf. Toll, *Blacking Up: The Minstrel Show in Nineteenth-Century America*, p. 43.

[18] Wittke, op. cit., p. 26.

[19] Cf. Wilfried Mellers, *Music in a New Found Land: Themes and Developments in the History of American Music* (New York, 1965), p. 264.

Mr. T. RICE
THE ORIGINAL JIM CROW

world at the present are Victoria and Jim Crow"[20] Jim Crow is the first fixed stage character that was indispensable from the minstrel show. Other actors also slipped in the role of Jim Crow in the 1830s.

Rice wrote and collected other minstrel songs, which were based on traditional melodies of the black population. With these songs, he wrote little, vulgar extravaganzas with a simple structure which were called "Ethiopian Operas". Their contents had nothing to do with the fate of African-Americans, as the title of some songs show: "Are Women More Beautiful than Men", "On Love", "Adam and Eve" or "Women's Tongue".[21] Side blows on current events and social criticism are still missing in the first half of the 19th century. However, the skits were antecedents for buffooneries which were not missing in any later minstrel show. Rice did not join any minstrel group and he always acted as a soloist, mostly between the acts, even as the minstrel show was established as a genre in American theater. In 1860, Rice died and was hailed as a pioneer by his colleagues and successors.

A further stage figure of the minstrel show was Zip Coon, identified like Jim Crow with a corresponding song. In his song, the Battle of New Orleans as well as General Jackson is mentioned. That is the reason why the song is thought to be composed and written at the beginning of the 19th century. The date however is not proven. This song was presented in 1834 in New York by Bob Farrell between two acts.

> Ole Zip Coon he is a larned skolar
> Stings 'posum up a gum tree an' coony in a holler.
> 'Posumup a gum tree, Coony on a stump.

---

[20] Dale Cockrell, *Demons of Disorder: Early Blackface Minstrels and Their World* (Cambridge, 1997), p. 66.

[21] Wittke, op. cit., p. 170.

Den over dubble trubble, Zip Coon will jump.[22]

"Zip Coon" was accompanied by a dance which is very similar to a rapid

---

[22] Wittke, op. cit., p. 180.

gigue.[23] This dance was popular especially with the skippers. The minstrel songs were passed on orally and were therefore, of course, not resistant against changes.

There were various models for the minstrel types. Composers and minstrels took the songs and the dialects of the plantation workers. They were imitated and even caricatured. The "swagger" was taken from the frontiersmen and from the steamboat darkies. Also their songs were taken for the minstrel show. Sources for minstrel numbers were also their tall-tales and adventure stories. Until the 1840s, white comedians in blackface appeared on stage between the acts of a play or they were part of a circus program.

[23] Cf. ibid., p. 17.

# 3. Banjo Music and Dance

In the 1820s and the 1830s, there were only Jim Crow and Zip Coon as the only re-occurring constituents of the minstrel show. They were accompanied by a small orchestra, a combo or just a violin. In the 1840s, a soloist was added accompanying himself on the banjo. The banjo player took the habit of blacks to beat the clock with the foot. When performing, a banjoist in the circus played on a wooden platform, so that the clock hit with the foot got more resonance.

The banjo is an instrument from Jamaica, which was introduced to North America in the seventeenth century. It was most popular among the blacks and it is a further development of the African banjar.[24] Initially, the banjo had only four strings, but later a fifth string known as "thumb string" was added in about 1845. The banjo was originally not a harmony instrument, but the banjoist played only the melody as the sound fades very quickly. The "thumb string" allowed a richer and peculiar harmony with a recurring accompanying score.[25] Ben Cotton learned from Negro slaves how to play the banjo: "From somewhere, perhaps from sessions such as these, banjo tunes with complex rhythms, that had no European antecedents and showed strong evidence of African polyrhythms, emerged in minstrelsy in the 1840s. These few dozen syncopated banjo tunes may have been the first evidence of the evolution of American jazz from the interaction of European melodies with African rhythms."[26] The song "Hams Banjo" is about the popularity of the banjo, which replaced the violin as the

---

[24] Cf. Mellers, op. cit., p. 266.

[25] Cf. Nathan, op. cit., p. 191.

[26] Toll, *Blacking Up: The Minstrel Show in Nineteenth-Century America*, p. 46.

predominant instrument in the minstrel show. Wittke writes about the "battle between banjo and violin": "Go way fiddle! folks is tired hearing you squawkin' / Keep silent for your betters – don't you hear de banjo talkin'?"[27] He also cites some self-reflexive songs:

> Loud de banjo talked away
> […]
> But when Dan Tucker touched his string,
> He'd make him shake like a locust's wing.[28]

Another song which illustrates the popularity of the banjo is the following:

> Den hand de Banjo down to play
> We'll make it ring both night and day
> And we care not what de white folks say,
> Dey can't get us to run away.[29]

In addition to the banjo player, also a soloist with his capers and body rotations was added. The Negro slaves in the Southern States observed by famous dancers were taken as examples. These dancers were watching their

---

[27] Wittke, op. cit., p. 188.

[28] Ibid., p. 183.

[29] Toll, *Blacking Up: The Minstrel Show in Nineteenth-Century America*, p. 95.

movements and developed dances from their observations. These were movements with all physical commitment and the dancers threw their arms high, but later the dances were limited only to the foot and footwork of the dancing Negro slaves. Initially, each soloist danced his own individual dance with high endurance and high speed, as the time emerged the dance took on a characteristic shape of the jutting heels of the Negro slave caricatured by elevation and exposing the heels. In addition, the knees were bow-legged, outwardly pressed or angled and their hands were snapped off at

the right angles. The speed of spins and jumps in the dances of the minstrel show was characteristic.[30] The dances were a cultural conglomerate of Af-

---

[30] A famous dancer of the minstrel show was Juba, a black slave and thus no real minstrel, who could inspire his audience by whirling rotations and quick jumps (cf. Nathan, op. cit. 74). Juba knew the dances of the black slaves in the South as well as those of the free African-Americans in the North. Dancing African-Americans were quite popular in 19th century America. Washington Irving, for example, mentions the "Long Iceland Negroes" with their dances in *Salmagundi.*

rican-American folklore. Also the dances of the frontiersmen and the boat men, as well as English folk dances entered the dance repertoire of the minstrel show. After the Civil War, these wild dances were better choreographed and they became an antecedent of modern step dance.

The classical minstrel show was not established until 1843, but we can already speak of a formation of the genre before that date. For the time being, only couples were encountered on stage: a dancer who was also a comedian and a vocalist who accompanied himself on an instrument were the conventional stage couple. The minstrel pair caricatured the African-Americans with their broad grinning, their huge eyeballs and their body movements. A milestone in the development of the minstrel show was the Ethiopian Opera. Minstrel songs and dances of the minstrel, crude buffoonery and small burlesque were combined into a complete program. Ethiopian Operas parodied also operas and ballets. The female roles were taken over by men. Thomas D. Rice managed to popularize the individual constituents of the minstrel show, but Dan Emmett compiled these constituents to a feature-length program with his Virginia Minstrels.

# 4. Daniel D. Emmet and the Virginia Minstrels

The musical talent Daniel Decatur Emmett was born in Mount Vernon, Ohio, in 1815. He joined a circus troupe in 1835 and sang songs, accompanied on a banjo in blackface. With the troupe, he moved from place to place, his banjo numbers accompanied dancers. He also appeared in the ensemble before he performed his first own work – *Hard Times; A Negro Extravaganza* – in 1855. He even starred in this simple farce. Thus, for the play, namely a pact with "Belzebub, the Prince of Darkness", and the language, namely dialect, he adapted African-American folklore for the stage. Banned from banjo music and singing, the devil danced with a chair gluing on his leg.[31] German folk farces were examples for these shows. Dan Emmett was influenced by Thomas D. Rice. He enriched the minstrel show with farces, music and poems. His poetry bears witness to impressive poetics despite his elementary education:

> Blow away ye gentle breezes
> All among de common treeses,
> Dar I set long wid de muses,
> Mendin my old boots and shuses.[32]

So called "stump speeches", parodies on speeches during election campaigns, which politicians hold on wooden pedestals were also added to the minstrel show. It was a monologue by one actor of the minstrel groups containing also philosophical topics. Typical of these dialogues were the use of malapropisms, incorrectly used foreign words, breaks and illogical conclusions, as the following example shows:

> Transcendentalism is dat spiritual cognoscence ob psychology irrefragibility, connected wid conscientient ademption ob incolumbient spirituality and etherialized connection — which is deribed from a profound contemplation

[31] Cf. ibid., p. 220.

[32] Ibid. p. 2.

> ob de irregability ob dose incessimable divisions ob de more minute portions ob subdivided particles ob inwisible atoms dat become ana-tom-ically tattable in de circumambulatin commotion ob ambiloquous vluminiousness.[33]

Dan Emmett's oeuvre represents a historically important contribution to 19th century popular theater in America.

In New York, Emmett met three like-minded actors: Frank Brower, Bill Whitlock and Dick Pelham. Together they founded the Virginia Minstrels in 1843. They sat in a semicircle. In the middle sat Emmett with a violin, besides him a banjo player and outside at the corner a tambourine player and a bones player.[34] The tambourine player and the bones player were called "endmen" or "cornermen". The white actors in blackface spoke an exaggerated form of black vernacular English. Their first minstrel show – *Ethiopian Concert* (1843) – consisted of two acts. Often, they just sang one number, the famous "Old Dan Tucker". It is a minstrel song about the life of the African-American: "A Virginian Refrain in which is described the ups and downs of Negro Life."[35] A lecture by an African-American about railways marked the end of the first part. The second part consisted of some more songs. One famous song with a dance was "De Boatman's Dance". *The New York Herald* writes about the first show by the Virginia Minstrels: "First Night of the novel, grotesque, original, and surprisingly melodious Ethiopian band, entitled the *Virginia Minstrels*, being an exclusively musical entertainment combining the banjo, violin, bone castanets, and tambourine, and entirely exempt from the vulgarities and other objec-

---

[33] Toll, *Blacking Up: The Minstrel Show in Nineteenth-Century America*, p. 70.

[34] "Bones" are castanets which really existed of bone originally.

[35] Nathan, op. cit., p. 119.

DANDY JIM FROM CAROLINE.
Nº1.
EMMIT'S
CELEBRATED
NEGRO MELODIES,
OR SONGS OF THE VIRGINNY BANJOIST
AT ALL THE PRINCIPAL THEATRES BY
D. D. EMMIT.
LONDON, D'ALMAINE & Cº 20. SOHO SQUARE
OLD DAN TUCKER. 2
WALK ALONG JOHN. 2
MY OLD AUNT SALLY 2
BOATMAN'S DANCE 2
COPYRIGHT.

tionable features which have hitherto characterized negro extravaganza."[36] The lack of obscenity was a characteristic feature of the minstrel show. It even was a competitive advantage compared to the variety show, thus in the 1860s the minstrel show was entertainment for the whole family, which was its advantage while competing with other genres of American theater.

In 1845, the Ethiopian Serenaders replaced the popularity of the Virginia Minstrels. Edwin Pearce Christy together with his composer Stephen Foster founded Christy's Minstrels, surpassing even the Ethiopian Serenaders. Whereas the shows of the Virginia Minstrels still consisted of two acts, the later classic minstrel show, created by E. P. Christy, consisted of three parts.[37] The first part was a series of minstrel songs and music. The second part was an olio, a number program, in which short farces and dances were played. Troupes offered parodies of European-style entertainment. The third part was a burlesque, later this was replaced by music hall performances. The burlesque were Shakespeare parodies, such as "Hamlet the Dainty", "Bad Breath, the Crane of Chowder", "Julius Sneezer" or "Dars-de-Money".[38] The last part was a further development of the Ethiopian Operas. In the 1850s, it was a "one-cat skit almost invariably set on southern plantations" with a potpourri of songs and dances, which were linked through dialogs.[39]

The Virginia Minstrels found several imitators, so that only the best could prevail. After their success in New York, the Virginia Minstrels went

---

[36] *New York Herald*, February 6-11, 1843 quoted in: ibid., p. 118.

[37] Cf. Glenn Hughes, *A History of the American Theatre 1700-1950* (New York, 1951), p. 331.

[38] Cf. Lott, op. cit., p. 75. Cf. William J. Mahar, "Ethiopian Skits and Sketches: Contents and Contexts of Blackface Minstrelsy, 1840-1890" (Middletown, 1996), p. 187.

[39] Toll, *Blacking Up: The Minstrel Show in Nineteenth-Century America*, p. 56.

on a tour through England which inspired other minstrel troupes to give guest tours from coast to coast. They also toured Europe and that in their absence allowed their competitors to establish themselves in the United States. After their tour of England, the Virginia Minstrels split up and Emmett joined other existing minstrel groups. He founded new troupes. He directed a theater in Chicago. He wrote new minstrel songs; "Dixie" is his best known song he wrote for the Bryant's Minstrels in 1859.

In New York's African Grove Theater Shakespeare's dramas were already performed by free blacks in 1821. However, these performances were quickly banned. African-Americans on the American stage were for a long time undesirable. In the 1840s and 1850s, however, they were artistically and financially promoted in shows by whites who wanted to see them in minstrel shows.[40] William Henry Lane and Thomas Dolward are two famous black minstrel performers. The "endmen" of this minstrel troupe were not black enough and so they had to blackface themselves like their white colleagues: "the end men were each rendered thoroughly black by burnt cork."[41] Even their advertisements played on stereotypes represented by black minstrel performers: "SEVEN SLAVES just from Alabama, who are EARNING THEIR FREEDOM by giving concerts under the guidance of their northern friends."[42] Even black minstrel performers kept to the racy stereotypes. This may be an indication that the contents and the representations of the minstrel show were not taken seriously. It was entertainment.

---

[40] Cf. ibid., p. 201.

[41] Ibid., p. 200.

[42] Ibid., p. 201.

CHRISTY'S MELODIES
AS COMPOSED AND SUNG BY THEM,
AT THEIR CONCERTS WITH DISTINGUISHED SUCCESS.
Edwin P. Christy

MECHANICS' HALL
472
BROADWAY, ABOVE GRAND STREET.
OPEN EVERY NIGHT
FRONT SEATS INVARIABLY RESERVED FOR LADIES
BRYANT'S
MINSTRELS
Bryant Brothers Proprietors and Managers
MONDAY EVENING, APRIL 4th, 1859
PROGRAMME—PART FIRST.
Instrumental Overture Bryant's Minstrels
Company
Jerry Bryant
J. Unsworth
Company
Dan Bryant
Full Band
Violin Solo
Tambourine Duet Jerry and Dan Bryant
Favorite Ballad Little Arthur
WE COME FROM THE HILLS
Neil Bryant
BURLESQUE ITALIAN OPERA
Local Banjo Song J. Unsworth
Wooden Shoe Dance
PLANTATION SONG AND DANCE,
DIXIE'S LAND
Introducing the whole Troupe in the Festival Dance.
"OUR AMERICAN COUSIN" BILL
NOTICE CHANGE OF TIME.
ADMISSION 25 CENTS

## 5. The Hey-Day of the Minstrel Show

The 1850s were the hey-day of the minstrel show: "The only places of amusement where the entertainments are indigenous are the African Opera Houses, where native American vocalists, with blackened faces, sing national songs, and utter none but native witticisms. These native theatricals ... are among the best frequented and most profitable places of amusement in New York. [...] the Ethiopian Opera has flourished like a green bay tree."[43] Other theatrical genres had to compete with the minstrel show, because audiences went to the minstrel show. It is no wonder, because in the middle of the 19th century the slave issue and the social status of African-Americans were at debate: "It was no accident that blackface entertainment dominated American show business in the middle decades of the nineteenth century when slavery, the plantation system, and the proper place of the Negro in America were the most important public issues, issues that challenged both the nation's democratic creed and its continued existence as one country."[44]

As with the circus, the minstrel troupe came into town with a parade led by a brass band in colorful costumes – white trousers, striped shirts and blue tailcoats. In the 1850s, the minstrel troupes were usually more than a dozen and rarely a quartet. Often a small delegation was sent to town before the whole troupe followed, so that they could learn what was new in town and what bothered its inhabitants. They included their experiences and the news they learned into their programs. Comedy and farce became more and more important for the minstrel show. Thus, the two "endmen",

---

[43] *Putman's Monthly* February 1854 quoted in: Nathan, op. cit., p. 218.

[44] Robert C. Toll, *On with the Show* (New York, 1976), p. 84.

Mr. Tambo and Mr. Bones, made funny faces and joked together including puns. Minstrel humor was simple and relied on slapstick and wordplay. The better jokes were reserved for the first minstrel, who presented these in his monologue. In addition to local color, the behavior of the African-American was still caricatured. The minstrels made fun of their superstition or their low and limited perception. In the 1850s, also anthologies with minstrel songs, "plantation melodies" or "Ethiopian choruses" and "minstrel joke books" were published.

In the 1850s, the minstrel show had conventionally three parts: an olio, a fantasia and a burlesque with a "walk around". The group sat in a semicircle at the ends, the two "endmen", also called "cornermen", who were still Mr. Tambo and Mr. Bones. The size of the troupe made it necessary that a master of ceremonies, known as Mr. Interlocutor, led through the shows while joking with the two "endmen". After the actors entered, Mr. Interlocutor opened the show with the words "Gentlemen, be seated!" and he introduced the troupe. In contrast to the minstrels with blackened faces, Mr. Interlocutor did not blackface himself and he did not wear a wig with curled hair. But like the rest of the troupe, he also sat in the semicircle. He had to know the whole show by heart, because he had to help out, if necessary as a prompter. Also, props decorated the stage in the 1850s. Previously, there were only four chairs for the Virginia Minstrels, now cabins and bales of cotton as symbols of the Southern States were added to the stage. The audience of the minstrel show was meant to believe that the Southern States is the home of the African-American, as it is expressed in songs where ex-slaves sang about their homesickness for the South. An idealized life on the plantations was presented to the public. In 1853, the Tom shows came up. It was a show within the third part of the minstrel show which was an adaptation of Harriett Beecher Stowe's novel *Uncle*

*Tom's Cabin.* In a joyous atmosphere a slapstick number "Happy Uncle Tom" or "Uncle Dad's Cabin" was presented to play down the racism involved in the minstrel show.[45] There were also parodies which criticized Stowe. The blacks were portrayed as happy people.

> Oh, white folks, we'll have you know
> Dis am not the version of Mrs. Stowe;
> Wid her de Darks am all unlucky
> But we am de boys from Old Kentucky.[46]

The minstrel show was double-edged: on the one hand, racism in the United States was reinforced; on the other hand, so many white Americans have come aware of black popular culture. No wonder therefore, the rise of the minstrel show coincided with the growth of the abolitionist movement. But without doubt, racial discrimination was played down in the minstrel show.

The minstrel show is a "distinctive American institution".[47] Their themes are linked to America and its history. In early minstrel songs, the Negro slave sang about special situations. The Negro slave was caricatured as he was perceived by the whites with their special features and characteristics, and what was typical for the whites. "The Gal from the South" is a song that expresses such a stereotypical perception:

> Ole Massa owned a colored girl –
> He bought her at the South;
> Her hair it curled so very tight;
> She could not shut her mouth.
> Her eyes they were so very small,
> They both ran into one,
> And when a fly lit in her eye,
> 'Twas like a June-bug in the sun.[48]

---

[45] Cf. Lott, op. cit., p. 211.

[46] Toll, *Blacking Up: The Minstrel Show in Nineteenth-Century America*, p. 95.

[47] Wittke, op. cit., p. 5.

[48] Quoted in: ibid., p. 186.

Another example is a joke with a racist background: "my girl has lips so large a lover could not kiss them all at once."[49] The fate of the Negro slave was the dominant theme in minstrel songs. Later the representation of human feelings was added.[50] An example of this is the excerpt from the following song:

> Lightning is a yaller gal, who libs up in de clouds,
> Thunder is a brack man, and he can holler loud,
> When he kisses Lightning, she darts up in a wonder,
> He jumps up and grabs de clouds and dat's what makes it thunder.[51]

The songs consist of simple poetics and the jokes are flat. Minstrel entertainment was popular: "The songs, the humor, the dances, and the instruments of the plantation darkies formed the nucleus out of which grew the first distinctly type of theatrical entertainment. Granted that the minstrel-show 'darky' was a caricature of the Negro; yet the caricature could not have been created without the original model, however great the subsequent distortion."[52] Minstrelsy was no folklore, but without the folklore of African-Americans they could not arise.[53]

Hans Nathan writes in his study about the complex formation of minstrelsy. The songs were actually English, Scottish or Irish folk melodies, which became folk songs in the South and were then adopted by the plantation workers because the Negro slaves were forbidden to practice their African folk music.[54] The songs of European origin were then acquired by slaves on the plantations and were transformed by African-Americans be-

---

[49] Toll, *Blacking Up: The Minstrel Show in Nineteenth-Century America*, p. 67.

[50] Cf. Wittke, op. cit., p. 39.

[51] Quoted in: ibid. p. 185.

[52] Chase, op. cit., p. 266.

[53] Cf. Wittke, op. cit., p. 174.

[54] Cf. Megan Sullivan, "African-American Music as Rebellion: From Slavesong to Hip-hop." (2001), p. 25.

fore minstrels discovered them again and in turn adapted them for the American stage. Minstrelsy thus originated a mêlée between the cultures of whites and blacks.[55] The African-American had a strong sense for rhythms, a great ability to improvise, as well as the willingness to assimilate property of a foreign culture to create songs which differed from those of the whites. The whites picked these songs up again from the plantation workers, impersonated their dialects, and caricatured their movements. What the minstrels adopted became the main component of minstrel shows.[56] "Dixie" is one such example for a song that has become a successful minstrel song by

Dan Emmett derived from an English folk song by the improvisation of Negro slaves. "Dixie" became popular on the minstrel stage at a time, when the question of slavery was at its peak. The lyrics and the melody catch the sharpness of the political unrest, moved by these also into ridiculousness. The same is true for the music and the dance accompanying the song. The song became the anthem of the Southern States during the Civil War, and was sung by the army of the Northern States with different lyrics. With its symbolism, the lyrics became the Confederate war anthem. In the Northern

---

[55] Also the used instruments were a blend of cultures: Banjo and tambourine are African instruments, violin and castanets are European instruments.

[56] Cf. Nathan, op. cit., p. 186. Cf. also Chase, op. cit., p. 121. Cf. also Cockrell, op. cit., p. 86.

States, people sang "Dixie for the Union" or "Dixie Unionized" instead. Comedians also used the song and altered it with their own verses.

Another important minstrel is the famous composer Stephen Foster, whose most popular minstrel songs besides "Oh, Susanna" are "Old Folks at Home", "My Old Kentucky Home" and "Massa's in the Cold Cold Ground". He actually wrote lyrical and sentimental songs for the middle class, but with minstrel songs he could express more sentimentality and more vitality. Foster lived in Cincinnati, where Negro slaves fled to the North along the Mississippi River and where frontiersmen departed to the West. In Cincinnati, he came across the songs of southern Negro slaves, who worked in the ports. He was inspired by the rhythm and the spirituality of the songs of the African-American.

With the outbreak of the Civil War, minstrels remained neutral. Minstrels put on patriotic numbers depicting scenes from American history or lionized figures like George Washington and Andrew Jackson in their shows. Social commentary became important. Most troupes added spirituals, known as jubilees, to their programs. By the 1870s, jubilees entered the repertoire, marking the first undeniably black music in the minstrel show.

## 6. The Decline of the Minstrel Show

During the Civil War, the minstrel show came to its decline. The troupes became larger. The J. H. Haverly's United Mastodon Minstrels, for example, had over 100 actors.[57] The set took greater proportions. The program was extensive: even Japanese acrobats and circus performers appeared in these shows. Each manager promised to offer the best show. The minstrel show was commercial entertainment and it developed into show business. The minstrel troupes destroyed each other, because they tried to be better and more extravagant than the others and thus they were no longer profitable and could not bear the spectacular shows. To attract more people to the monster shows, it fell back on vulgar entertainment.

[57] Cf. Watkins, op. cit., p. 98.

Around the year 1870, the classic minstrel show was extinct. Less frequently, performers blackened their faces, but instead music hall numbers entered the minstrel show with Harlequins and bad jokes. It was no longer claimed to imitate the southern Negro.

> There was an ever-widening gap between the mimicry of pre-Civil War days, with its typical, simple Negro songs and dances, and the "Punch and Judy costumes", "stale newspaper jokes", and the "mere foolish and unmeaning cackle" of later years. Caricaturing supplanted carefully studied plantation types, and sentimental ballads of every description, parodies, and clog dances drove from the program such themes and melodies as Emmett's "Old Dan Tucker", while coarse comedy replaced the whimsical humor of old Negro types.[58]

In retrospect, an "old trouper", a minstrel singer from the older generation, described the decline of the traditional minstrel show in 1929: "The Southern atmosphere got lost. It gave way to the mixing of chorus girls in the show, and the minstrelsy became musical comedy, 'corked up', and billed as minstrelsy."[59] The shows were still called minstrel shows, even if they lacked their original generic features. For example, the minstrels encountered in the 1870s no longer had colored faces. The inclusion of actresses in the minstrel show is responsible for the decline into cheap "girl shows". In 1870, Madame Rentz's female minstrels grew to an eleven-member troupe of women.[60] All this led to the decline of the minstrel show. The decline started in the cities. The traveling minstrels in the provinces, mostly smaller troupes, were able to continue up to the 20th century.

Competition with other genres of theater – vaudeville, burlesque, musical comedy backed by master promoters like P. T. Barnum – and with the movie industry led up to the decay. The audience wanted to see even better

---

[58] Wittke, op. cit., p. 121.

[59] Quoted in: ibid., p. 123.

[60] Cf. Toll, *Blacking Up: The Minstrel Show in Nineteenth-Century America*, p. 142.

shows. "Big Business" was not just a slogan of American economy, but was also a slogan of American theater. In musical comedy higher fees were paid than in the minstrel show, so that many of their stars were recruited. The cost of production increased so much so that the minstrel show was no longer profitable. The audience in the "roaring twenties" wanted to see shows with strong sex appeal, but the minstrel show could not appeal. Also African-Americans formed minstrel troupes, such as Sam Hague's Slave Troupe of Georgia Minstrels.[61] They tried on the minstrel show and formed the so-called "all Negro shows". Glenn Hughes writes: "There were a few colored troupes – the first of which appeared in the seventies – but none of them attained the prestige of popularity of the best white companies. And,

[61] Cf. Watkins, op. cit., p. 109.

so strong was the blackface tradition of the minstrel show that even the colored performers covered their faces with burnt cork whether they needed it or not."[62] As a result, white actors with their blackened faces lost their appeal. In 1919, there were only three minstrel troupes of rank. More amateur troupes used this kind of entertainment, as well. The stars of the minstrel show were singers in vaudeville, in the musical, as well as in movies, such as Al Jolson starring successfully in *The Jazz Singer* (1927). When the A. G. Field Minstrels broke up in 1928, it marks the end of the genre.

[62] Hughes, op. cit., p. 312.

# 7. The Cultural Importance of the Minstrel Show and Its Legacy

For the development of American musical theater, the music of the minstrel show was important. In his book on America's music Gilbert Chase shows how jazz, in particular blues, evolved from minstrelsy and ragtime.[63] Ragtime was inspired by "cakewalk". "Cakewalk" is a dance competition among Negro slaves; the slave-owner gave a cake as a prize for the best dancer. Ragtime is a fusion of white minstrelsy and African-American folk music with European techniques. Ragtime is not improvised, it is composed. Because of published compositions, ragtime emerged in the cities. Minstrel music could only develop, because Negro slaves in the Mississippi Basin had enough freedom to improvise syncopated and polyrhythmic music during and after their work on the cotton plantations. With this music the Negro slaves could express themselves on stage. The fateful community of whites and blacks meant that the whites impersonated the blacks in the minstrel show and the blacks imitated the whites in their "cakewalks".

In his book *Dan Emmett and the Rise of the Early Negro Minstrelsy*, Hans Nathan sees the origin of jazz in the Minstrel's banjo music.[64] Already the early minstrel used hectic accentuations against the main stresses of the bar that led, finally, to the use of syncopated tunes. By piling up counter stresses the vital and rhythmic music of the banjo pieces were developed. Also the minstrel knew the possibility to put through the strict bar of the melody by irregular blows as it was usual in 20th century jazz. An-

---

[63] Cf. Chase, op. cit., p. 121. Cf. also Cockrell, op. cit., pp. 496 ff.

[64] Cf. Nathan, op. cit., pp. 209 ff.

other inheritance of the minstrel for jazz, especially for blues, is the low-spirited mood which was often expressed by minor harmonies.

Another contribution of the minstrel show for the development of American musical theater was the enrichment of the American song. An example is Stephen Foster's "Old Folks at Home" titled "Swanee River" in the original. George Gershwin fell back on this minstrel song and entitled his version "Swanee" that only became popular by the interpretation of Al Jolson in *Sindbad* (1918). Also Marion Cook adopted constituents of the minstrel show for the African-American operetta *Clorindy; the Origin of the Cakewalk* (1898). Cook substituted the conventional three beats to the bar with ragtime rhythms and allowed a choir which existed only of African-Americans to appear on stage. High-class African-American dancers, "cakewalking like angels, black angels",[65] let the show look authentic.

Robert C. Toll evaluates the importance of the minstrel show for American show business: "The Minstrel Show was the first uniquely American show business form. As the most popular entertainment form in the nation for a half-century, it had a great impact on vaudeville, burlesque and its other show business successors."[66] Vaudeville, burlesque and revue started the succession of the minstrel show in America as dominating theatrical genres before the American musical achieved its breakthrough in the 1920s. Ragtime, blues and jazz which were also developed within the minstrel show flowed directly into the American musical as firm constituents. Also the light wordplays of the minstrel show were found in vaudeville and in the revue. Veterans of the minstrel show – George Thatcher, Al Jolson, Frank Tinney and Eddie Cantor –, nevertheless, revived the old days nostalgically in the newer genres of American theater. Librettist and revue star George L. Cohan remembered the minstrel show in songs like "That Old-Fashioned Cakewalk" and "Two of Dandy Darkies". In *Hello Broadway* (1914), George M. Cohan appeared with a black colored face and also Ethel Barrymore played the leading role in *Scarlet Sister Mary* (1930) with a black colored face as homage to former times of American theater. George M. Cohan and Ethel Barrymore were the only exceptions in blackface who tried to revive the minstrel show in the 20th century.

---

[65] Cecil Smith and Glenn Litton, *Musical Comedy in America* (New York, 1981), p. 128.

[66] Toll, *On with the Show*, p. 81.

# 8. Bibliography

Bauch, Marc. *The American Musical*. Marburg: Tectum Verlag, 2003.

---. *Themes and Topics of the American Musical after World War II*. Marburg: Tectum Verlag, 2001.

Cantwell, Robert. *Bluegrass Breakdown: The Making of the Old Southern Sound*. Chicago: University of Illinois Press, 1984.

Chase, Gilbert. *America's Music*. New York: McGraw-Hill, 1955.

Cockrell, Dale. *Demons of Disorder: Early Blackface Minstrels and their World*. Cambridge: Cambridge University Press / Cambridge Studies in American Theatre and Drama, 1997.

Hughes, Glenn. *A History of the American Theatre 1700-1950*. New York: French, 1951.

Jackson, Ronald L. *Scripting the Black Masculine Body: Identity, Discourse, and Racial Politics in Popular Media*. Albany: State University of New York Press, 2006.

Lott, Eric. *Love and Theft: Blackface Minstrelsy and the American Working Class*. New York: Oxford University Press, 1993.

Mahar, William J. "Ethiopian Skits and Sketches: Contents and Contexts of Blackface Minstrelsy, 1840-1890." *Inside the Minstrel Mask: Readings in Nineteenth-Century Blackface Minstrelsy*. Eds.: Annemarie Bean, James V. Hatch und Brooks McNamara. Middletown: Wesleyan University Press, 1996.

Malone, Bill C., and David Stricklin, *Southern Music / American Music*. Lexington: University Press of Kentucky, 2003.

Marc, David. *Comic Visions: Television Comedy & American Culture*. Malden, Massachusetts: Blackwell Publishers Inc., 1997.

Mellers, Wilfried. *Music in a New Found Land: Themes and Developments in the History of American Music*. New York: Oxford University Press, 1965.

Nathan, Hans. *Dan Emmett and the Rise of Early Negro Minstrelsy*. Norman: University of Oklahoma Press, 1962

Oliver, Paul. *The Story of the Blues*. Harmondsworth: Penguin, 1972.

Paskman, Dailey, and Sigmund Spaeth. *Gentlemen, Be Seated!* Garden City: Doubleday, Doran & Company, 1928.

Sacks, Howard L., and Judith Sacks. *Way up North in Dixie: A Black Family's Claim to the Confederate Anthem.* Washington: Smithsonian Institution Press, 1993.

Smith, Cecil, and Glenn Litton. *Musical Comedy in America.* New York: Theatre Arts Books, 1981.

Sotiropoulos, Karen. *Staging Race: Black Performers in Turn of the Century America.* Cambridge: Harvard University Press, 2006.

Sullivan, Megan. "African-American Music as Rebellion: From Slavesong to Hip-hop." *Discoveries* 3: (2001): 21–39.

Toll, Robert C. "Behind the Blackface: Minstrel Men and Minstrel Myths." *American Heritage* 29 (1978): 3.

---. *Blacking Up: The Minstrel Show in Nineteenth-century America.* New York: Oxford University Press, 1974.

---. *On with the Show.* New York: Oxford University Press, 1976.

Watkins, Mel. *On the Real Side: Laughing, Lying, and Signifying—The Underground Tradition of African-American Humor that Transformed American Culture, from Slavery to Richard Pryor.* New York: Simon & Schuster, 1994.

Wald, Elijah. *Escaping the Delta: Robert Johnson and the Invention of the Blues.* New York: Amistad, 2004.

Wittke, Carl F. *Tambo and Bones: A History of the American Minstrel Stage.* Durham: Greenwood Press, 1930.

Woodward, C. Vann. *The Strange Career of Jim Crow.* New York: Oxford University Press, 1955.

## By the Same Author

Bauch, Marc. *Themes and Topics of the American Musical after World War II*. Edition Wissenschaft. Reihe Amerikanistik. Band 16. Marburg: Tectum Verlag, 2001

ISBN: 3-8288-1141-8

Bauch, Marc. *The American Musical*. Marburg: Tectum Verlag, 2003.

ISBN: 3-8288-8458-X

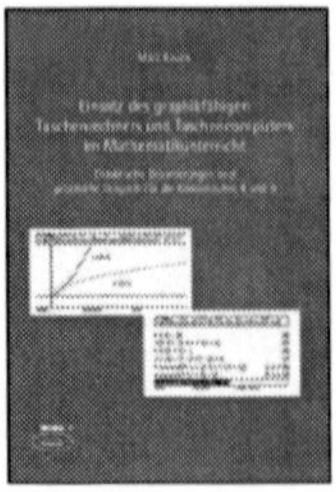

Bauch, Marc. *Einsatz des graphikfähigen Taschenrechners und Taschencomputers im Mathematikunterricht*. Stuttgart: Wiku-Verlag, 2004.

ISBN: 3-936749-37-X

Bauch, Marc. *Friar Lawrence's Plan in William Shakespeare's ROMEO AND JULIET and His Function as a Counsellor*. München: Grin, 2007.

ISBN: 978-3-638-77449-9

and many more …

## About the Author

Marc A. Bauch, born in Hermeskeil, Germany, in 1973

- studied Mathematics, American Literature and Computer Science at the University of Saarbrücken, the University of Hagen and the University of Glasgow
- taught Mathematics and American Literature at the University of Saarbrücken
- is involved in the support of young scientists participating in the "Jugend forscht" competition, was a judge for Mathematics and Computer Science and is now leading and managing the competition in Bitburg, Germany
- was an anchorman for „Univox – das saarländische Hochschulradio" and produced a documentary on the American Musical
- is a member of the Deutsche Gesellschaft für Amerikastudien and the Gesellschaft für Kanadastudien
- teaches Mathematics, English and Computer Science at Gymnasium Hermeskeil

**Publications**

*Themes and Topics of the American Musical after World War II* (Marburg, 2001)

*The American Musical* (Marburg, 2003)

*Einsatz des graphikfähigen Taschenrechners und Taschencomputers im Mathematikunterricht* (Stuttgart, 2004)

*Friar Lawrence's Plan in William Shakespeare's Romeo and Juliet and His Function as a Counsellor* (München, 2007)

*Teaching Grammar: Conditional Clauses* (München, 2007)

*Textarbeit mit kommunikativen Übungen* (München, 2007)

*Additionsverfahren: Algorithmus und Lösbarkeit* (München, 2007)

*Berühren und senkrechtes Schneiden von Funktionsgraphen* (München, 2007)

*Zahlbereichserweiterung durch Bruchteile* (München, 2007)

CPSIA information can be obtained at www.ICGtesting.com
Printed in the USA
BVOW022241280313

316771BV00001B/14/P

9 783656 086369